Published in the UK in 1994 by
Schofield & Sims Limited, Huddersfield, England.

0 7217 5003 6

Ships

Schofield & Sims Limited Huddersfield.

The Different Parts of a Ship

The tiller and the rudder, found at the back of a sailing-ship, are used to steer it.

Sailing-ships are powered by the wind which inflates the sail. In olden days, the clipper, which had many sails, was very fast.

Most sailing boats have a long, smooth hull to sail easily through the water. Some of them have two or three hulls.

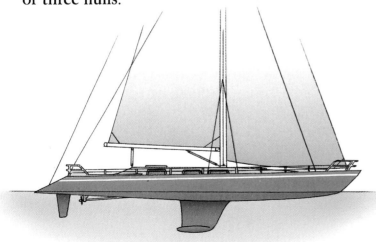

Today, many ships have huge engines. The engine turns the propellers.

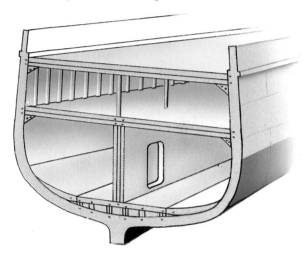

The hold is the part of the ship where cargo is stored.

The deck is the place where the passengers can walk about. Liners have several decks.

The pointed ends of the anchor catch on the seabed and stop the ship from moving.

Radar enables the captain to steer the ship safely even at night or in fog.

The First Boats

Boats have existed since very early times. Canoes and kayaks, often seen today, are not very different from some of the early boats.

One of the oldest boats was probably a raft made from tree-trunks. It was strong but no use for long journeys.

For speed, paddles replaced hands and sticks.

The first Egyptian boats were made from *reeds*. They were curved so that passengers did not get wet.

Eventually the sail was invented. Then it was the wind that made the boat move.

Fighting Ships

The first big ships used for exploring and conquering the world were also fighting ships, called galleys. On such ships, the oarsmen were usually slaves.

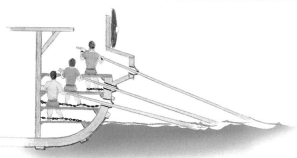

The trireme was a galley in which the oarsmen were seated on three levels. They were chained to their seats so that they could not escape.

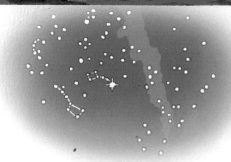

Navigators used the sun and the stars, particularly the Pole star, to find their way across the seas.

The long ship, nicknamed 'terror of the seas', made it possible for the *Vikings* to conquer many kingdoms. The ship was able to ride the storms on the high seas.

The *Reale* was one of the last galleys built. It was badly designed and the oarsmen often sat waist-deep in water.

The Galleon

The galleon was a huge sailing-ship which was used for travelling long distances across the oceans to look for treasure, such as gold or *spices*. It was armed with cannon.

Galleons had large crews. Men slept on *hammocks* or on the floor.

During the voyage, the sailors had to check the rigging and mend torn sails.

Because ships spent several months at sea, huge quantities of drink were taken on board, particularly water and beer. Live chickens, pigs and goats were also kept for fresh meat and milk during the voyage.

The Port

Ports are built to offer ships shelter and allow them to load and unload their cargoes. The larger ports have enormous warehouses for storing goods and huge *silos* for storing grain. They also have shipyards where boats are built or repaired.

Tugs are powerful little boats that pull large cargo ships in and out of the docks.

The fire boat is equipped to fight fires on board ships.

The lightship is a sort of floating lighthouse. These ships remain at sea even during stormy weather.

The lifeboat is used to save lives at sea. It is designed not to capsize.

Sailing-boats Today

These days, sailing-boats are mostly used for leisure and sport. There are races, called regattas, for small sailing-boats, that take place close to the shore. Round-the-world races are big sporting events.

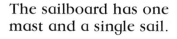

The sailboard has one mast and a single sail.

Some sailing-boats have several hulls to make them more steady. The catamaran has two hulls and the trimaran has three.

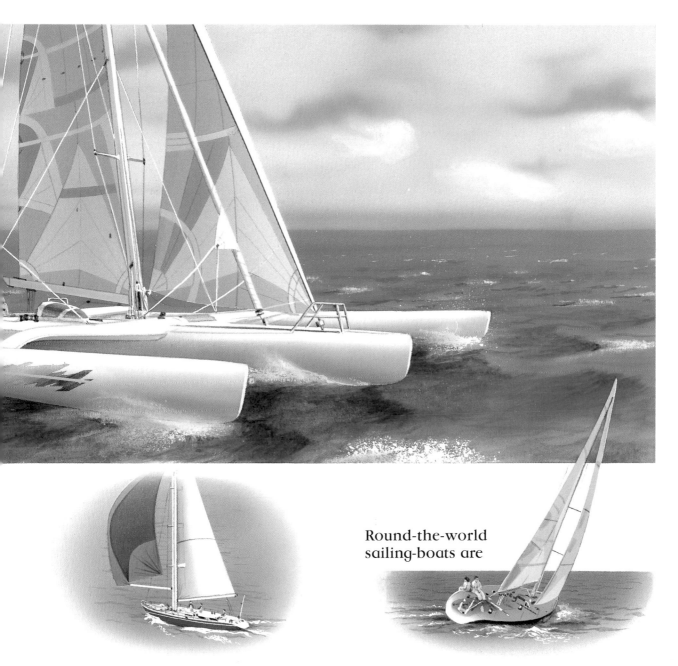

Round-the-world
sailing-boats are

This racing yacht sails faster, thanks to
a huge front sail – the spinnaker.

specially built and equipped to
withstand very rough weather.

Fishing Boats

Trawlers that go to fish distant waters are away from port for several days. Some large modern trawlers which can catch and *refrigerate* many tonnes of fish are away for several weeks.

Small fishing boats fish near to the coast. They return to harbour each evening.

There are factory ships on which fish are frozen or tinned during the fishing expedition.

Different fishing nets are used, depending on whether the fish feed near the surface or on the seabed.

Some fishing vessels have sonar which can locate shoals of fish 5 kilometres away.

15

Cargo Ships

The biggest ships are those which transport goods. The oil tanker, often called a supertanker, is the biggest ship of all.
Oil is stored in its huge tanks.

Some oil tankers are so big that they cannot get into port. The oil has to be unloaded from them by pipeline.

There are many container ships. Containers are large 'boxes' full of goods. Container ships are loaded and unloaded by giant cranes.

Some cargo ships are *refrigerated*. They carry – and keep fresh – meat, fruit and dairy products.

Other cargo vessels carry iron ore which can be turned into steel and used, among other things, for making cars.

Liners

Before the invention of aeroplanes, liners were the only way of transporting large numbers of people across seas and oceans.

The first liners were steam ships. They took 15 days to cross the Atlantic Ocean.

Liners have become more and more luxurious and can now cross the Atlantic Ocean in less than a week.

The modern luxury liner is like a small floating town, with shops, restaurants, sports facilities and cinemas.

Passengers have lots to do on a liner. Larger liners usually have swimming-pools.

Atlantic crossings could be dangerous. In 1912, the *Titanic*, a luxury liner, hit a huge iceberg and sank, with the loss of many lives.

Ferries

For short journeys, there are several types of boat, such as the ferry, which transport cars, lorries, coaches and even trains, as well as passengers.

Paddle-boats are sometimes used to ferry people along rivers or across lakes.

When the hydrofoil moves slowly, it moves like a boat in the water. At speed, it raises its hull out of the water and 'skis' across the surface.

The hovercraft carries passengers and cars. It crosses the sea on a cushion of air created by fans. It comes on land to load and unload.

In Venice, there are canals instead of streets. Some people travel in gondolas rowed by gondoliers.

21

Ships of War

The first ships used in war were sailing-vessels, like galleys. Today, warships are very powerful and can be huge, like aircraft carriers.

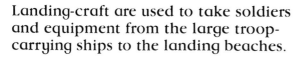

Landing-craft are used to take soldiers and equipment from the large troop-carrying ships to the landing beaches.

The minesweeper can locate mines and destroy them.

Destroyers carry helicopters, torpedoes and missiles. They also carry anti-aircraft weapons.

Other warships carry *depth-charges* to attack submarines.

Submarines

The first submarine was made out of wood. It could only carry one person. Today, submarines are capable of diving to enormous depths and of staying there for weeks at a time without coming back to the surface.

In a submarine, the periscope lets people see from under the water.

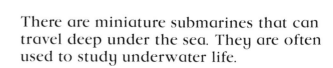

There are miniature submarines that can travel deep under the sea. They are often used to study underwater life.

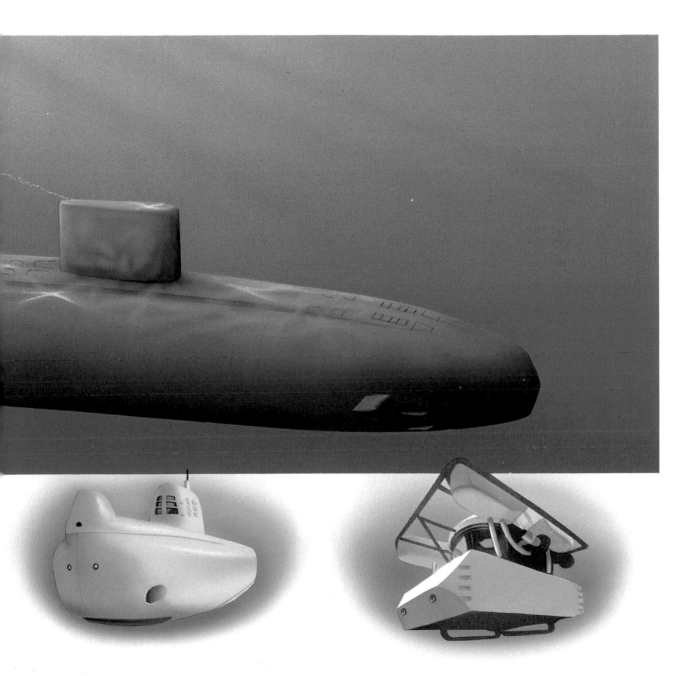

Some submarines carry divers to great depths so that they can repair cables or oil rigs.

This little submarine can locate *shipwrecks* and recover treasure.

Glossary

Depth-charge

A weapon of war, used as a bomb for destroying submarines.

Hammock

A suspended network of rope or canvas in which sailors used to sleep.

Reed

A tall, stiff plant that grows in water.

Refrigerate

To keep certain foods fresh by using cold air.

Shipwreck

A boat that has sunk.

Silo

A large tower where grain is stored.

Spice

Pepper, cinnamon, vanilla are spices. They are used to flavour foods.

Vikings

Long ago, the Vikings lived in the north of Europe. They were very good navigators.